Map Skills for Today

Grade 1

Finding Your Way

Map Skills for Today
Finding Your Way
Grade 1

Publisher: Keith Garton
Editorial Director: Maureen Hunter-Bone
Editorial Development: Summer Street Press, LLC
Writer: Judy Glickman
Project Editor: Miriam Aronin
Editor: Alex Giannini
Design and Production: Dinardo Design, LLC
Photo Editor: Kim Babbitt

Illustration Credits: Millicent Schaffer, Clive Scruton
Map Credits: Mapping Specialists, Ltd.
Photo Credits: Page 6: Super Stock; Page 7: John Klein/Weekly Reader; Page 8: Masterfile, Corbis, Erica Shires/zefa/ Corbis; Page 26: Jupiter Images, Jochen Schlenker/Masterfile, Jupiter Images, J.A. Kraulis/Masterfile, Jimmy Chin/Getty Images, Hubert Stadler/Corbis

Teachers: Go online to www.scholastic.com/mapskillsfortoday for teaching ideas and the answer key.

ISBN: 978-1-338-21487-1

3 4 5 6 7 8 9 10   40   23 22 21 20

Finding Your Way

Table of Contents

What Is a Map?

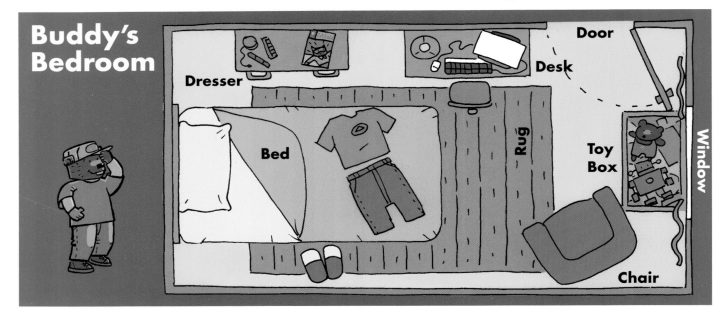

Buddy's Bedroom

Dresser — Desk — Door — Bed — Rug — Toy Box — Window — Chair

Dear Girls and Boys,

A **map** is a drawing of a place. It shows where things are. A map looks as if someone drew it from high up. Pretend I am drawing a map of my bedroom from high up.

Your friend,

Buddy

✶ Use Your Skills

Circle the word that tells where things are.

1. The bed is on the _____.

   rug   dresser

2. The toy box is next to the _____.

   window   desk

Map It!

Now think about your own bedroom. Where is your bed? Where is your window? What else is in your bedroom?

Draw a map of your bedroom in the box below. Remember to write a title for your map.

Title

What Does Earth Look Like?

Dear Boys and Girls,

Someday I'd like to be a spacebear. I will go up, up, into space! Then I will look down at Earth. **Earth** is the planet we live on.

Look at the picture of Earth. It was taken from space. You can see that Earth is round like a ball. You can also see that it has land areas and lots and lots of water.

Your friend,

Buddy

☆ Use Your Skills

Finish each sentence with a word from the box.

water	Earth	round

1. The planet we live on is called _____.

2. The shape of Earth is _____.

3. Earth has less land than _____.

What Is a Globe?

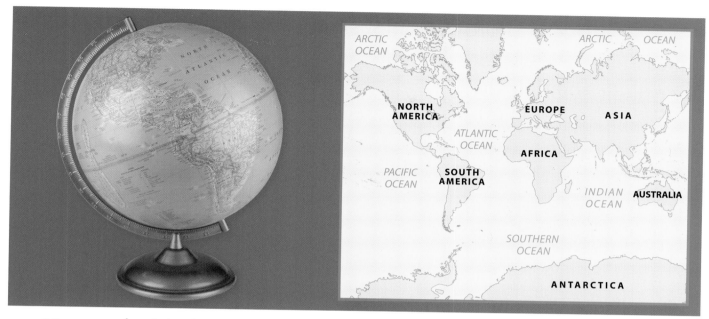

You probably have something in your classroom that is round like Earth. It is called a globe. A **globe** shows all of Earth. But you can only see half of Earth at one time on a globe.

A map, like the map of Buddy's bedroom, is flat. You can see the whole Earth at one time on a map.

☆ Use Your Skills

Draw a line under each true sentence.

1. A globe is round like Earth.

2. A globe shows things in your home.

3. You can see all of Earth at the same time on both a globe and a map.

👉 Your Turn Now

Look at the globe and the map. Circle the part of Earth on the map that you can see on the globe.

What Are Map Symbols?

A **symbol** is a drawing that stands for a real thing. Many maps use symbols to stand for real things. Look at the pictures and their symbols.

Use Your Skills

1. Circle the symbol of the tree.

2. Draw a line under the symbol of the swing.

3. Draw an **X** on the symbol of the slide.

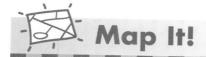

Symbols help you use a map. A map **key** tells you what the symbols on the map stand for.

Look at the symbols and the words that tell what they stand for. The symbols for house and ball are missing. Draw these symbols where they belong in the key.

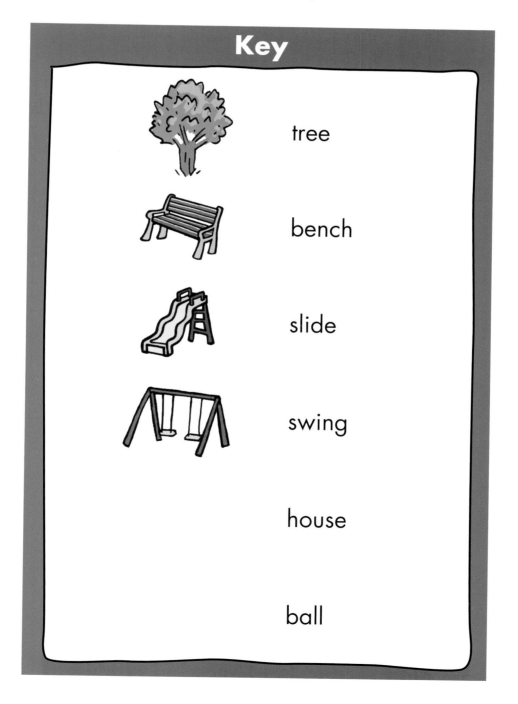

Use Map Symbols

Lake View Park

KEY

trees   rocks   fireplace   logs

lake   island   picnic table   tent

Buddy went to the park. He saw 🌲. He saw 🪨. Then he saw a big 🫘. Buddy put his toy boat into the 🫘. The boat sailed to an 🏝️.

⭐ Use Your Skills

Look at the key and the map. Find each symbol in the key on the map.

1. Draw an **X** on the lake.

2. Draw a circle around the rocks.

3. Draw a ✓ on the trees.

 **Map It!**

Dear Girls and Boys,

What a surprise! When I came back to the park, things were different. Some things were still there. Some things were missing. And some fun things had been added.

What things would you add to the park to make it fun for you? Please draw them for me on the map. Then add them to the key. Begin by adding back the lake and the island. They have been put in the key for you.

Your friend,

Buddy

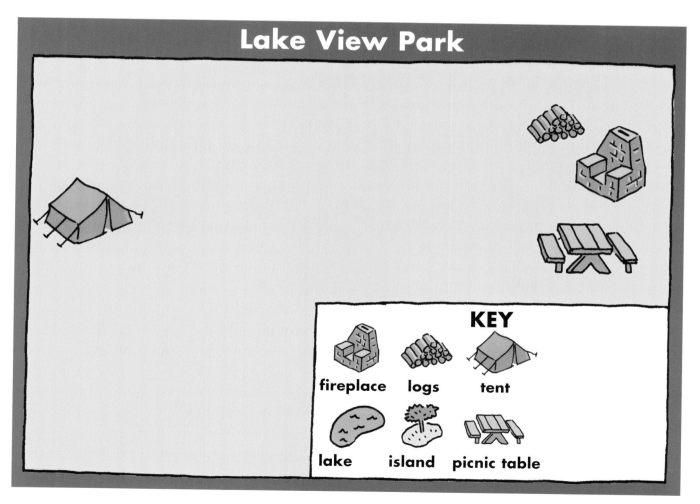

Follow the Symbols

Buddy's House

KEY

tree

Buddy

Momma Bear

bed

table

swing

Mouse

sandbox

Teddy Bear

🐻 was sad. It was time for 🛏️ . And 🐻 couldn't find his 🧸 . "I can't go to 🛏️ without my 🧸 ," said 🐻 . And one big tear rolled down his cheek.

"I'll help you find him," said 🐭 . "Let's think. Where was your 🧸 this morning?"

"He was on my [bed]," said [bear]. "Then we sat at the [table] to eat."

"Where did you take your [teddy] next?" asked [mouse].

"My [teddy] and I went to the [swing]," said [bear]. "Then I climbed a [tree] while the [teddy] sat under it. He can't climb, you know."

"Then what did you do?" asked [mouse]. "We played in the [sandbox]," said [bear]. "Then [dog] called me in for supper. And—I must have left my [teddy] in the [sandbox]."

[bear] and [mouse] ran out to the yard. And there was Buddy's [teddy] all alone in the [sandbox].

[bear] picked up his [teddy] and gave him a big hug. "I'm so glad I've found you," said [bear]. "Thank you, [mouse], for helping me. Now we can all go to bed!"

☆ Use Your Skills

Let's read the story again. This time follow Teddy Bear's trip by drawing a line with your black crayon from each place to the next during Buddy's day on the picture of Buddy's house on page 12. (HINT: Start your line from Buddy's bed.)

Near or Far?

Neighborhood Park

Maps can show you whether things are near or far away. Something that is **near** is close to you. Something that is **far** is a long way from you.

⭐ Use Your Skills

Circle the word that correctly answers the question.

1. Is Buddy **near** or **far** from the ball?

2. Find the bench. Is it **near** or **far** from the ball?

3. Is the sandbox **near** or **far** from the ball?

👉 Your Turn Now

Look around your classroom. Tell a partner some things that are near to you and far from you.

Find Places in Buddy's Neighborhood

Buddy's Neighborhood

Firehouse Avenue

Park

Church

Firehouse

Market

School

Offices

Park Road

Garden Street

School Street

Gas station

Library

Buddy's house

Green Road

Garden

Library Way

This is a map of Buddy's neighborhood. Some places are near his house. Other places are far away.

 **Use Your Skills**

Circle the word that tells which is nearer to Buddy's house.

1. **firehouse** or **school**   2. **library** or **park**

3. **church** or **gas station**

Draw a line under the word that tells which is farther away from Buddy's house.

4. **library** or **firehouse**   5. **market** or **park**

6. **offices** or **garden**

Left or Right?

LEFT   **RIGHT**

Buddy is visiting the Animal Park. He is trying to decide in which direction to walk. **Directions** tell us which way we want to go. Many kinds of unusual animals live in the Animal Park. Using the directions **left** and **right** will make it easy for Buddy to find them. Look at the drawing of Buddy. He is facing forward. You are facing the same direction. Put an X on his left side. Put a ✓ on his right side.

☆ Use Your Skills

Look at the map on page 17. Write the direction word **left** or **right** to tell which way Buddy should walk to get from animal to animal.

1.   to   _____

2.   to   _____

3.   to   _____

Animal Park

 ## Think It Over

Face the front of the classroom. Raise your right hand. Then raise your left hand. Now face the back of the classroom. Are your right and left hands in the same place?

 ## Your Turn Now

1. Put an **X** on the animal that is farther left.

   red elephant   green elephant

2. Circle the animal that is nearer to the right.

   bears   camel

Four Main Directions

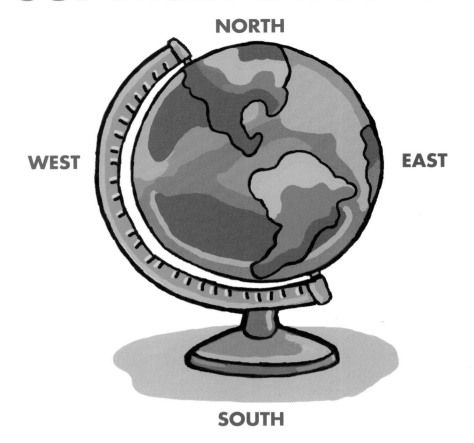

NORTH

WEST

EAST

SOUTH

Earth has four main directions. They are north, south, east, and west. You can see them on this drawing. **North** is the direction toward the North Pole. **South** is the direction toward the South Pole.

Now find east. When you face north, **east** is always to your right. **West** is always to your left.

 Think It Over

1. If you are facing south, what direction is behind you?

2. If you are facing east, what direction is to your left?

3. Which two directions are between north and south?

Use Directions on a Map

Animal Farm

Directions help you read maps. You can see that the sheep are in the east. Circle them. On what side of the farm are the pigs?

Use Your Skills

Write the direction word that tells which way to go to get from animal to animal.

| north | south | east | west |

1. 🐷🐷 to 🐕🐕 _____

2. 🐐 to 🐑🐑 _____

3. 🐔🐔 to 🐷🐷 _____

Visit Buddy's Neighborhood

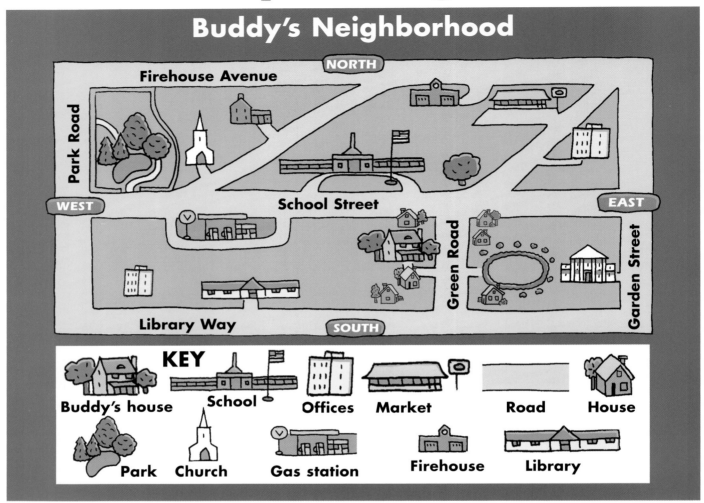

Buddy's Neighborhood

Here we are in Buddy's neighborhood again. This time the map has a key to tell you what the symbols stand for. Follow Buddy's route from his house to school. A **route** is a way to go from one place to another. Buddy leaves his house and turns north on Green Road. Use a black crayon to draw Buddy's route.

Think It Over

Buddy could also use other routes to go to school. Pretend Buddy turns south on Green Road. Use a red crayon to draw a different route he could take to school.

Find Buddy's Address

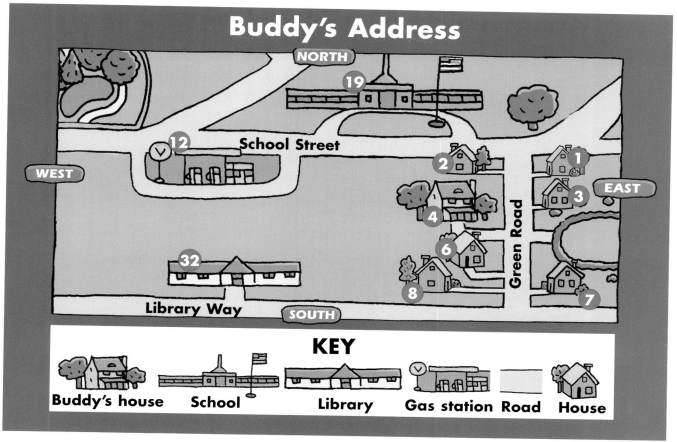

Buddy's Address

NORTH

19

School Street

12

WEST

2

1

EAST

4

3

Green Road

6

32

8

7

Library Way

SOUTH

KEY

Buddy's house   School   Library   Gas station   Road   House

Buddy's house has an address. So does yours. An **address** has a number and a street name. Find the gas station on the map. The address of the gas station is 12 School Street.

☆ Use Your Skills

1. Draw a ✓ on the school. What is its address?

_____

2. Circle the library. What is its address?

_____

3. Draw a ★ on Buddy's house. What is his address?

_____

Follow the Route to a Treasure

Treasure Map

Buddy was playing pirate. He was hunting for treasure. But he wasn't having any luck. And his tummy was growling. Buddy Bear was hungry!

Betsy Bee flew by. Betsy dropped something. Buddy picked it up. It was a treasure map!

Buddy began to follow the treasure map. He walked west to a stone wall. Betsy Bee was there. "Keep following the map," buzzed Betsy Bee.

So Buddy walked south and east to Blue Lake. There he walked across a long bridge. Buddy came to an island. Betsy Bee was there. "Keep following the map," buzzed Betsy Bee.

So Buddy walked up a hill. He went north and then east. At last he came to Long River. Then he walked east to a big rock. Buddy looked at the map again. He was near the treasure at last.

Buddy took 10 giant steps south. He saw an old tree with a hole in it. Buddy reached into the hole. There was the treasure. It was a big jar of HONEY!

"Yummy!" said Buddy. "Thank you, Betsy Bee. It's fun to find a treasure you can eat." And Buddy's tummy didn't growl anymore.

 **Your Turn Now**

Use a crayon to trace Buddy's route to find the treasure.

 **Map It!**

Dear Girls and Boys,

Let's make a treasure map together! I think our 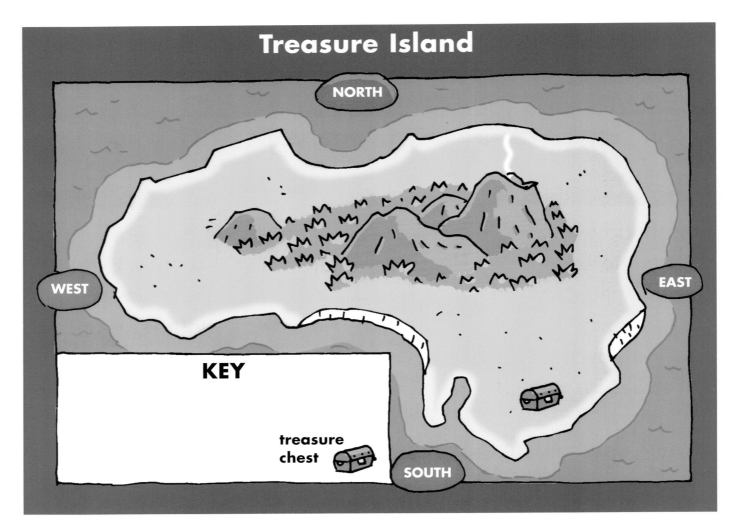 should be on an island. Now the rest is up to you. Decide what places to put on the island. Then draw symbols for them. Remember to show and label your symbols in the map key. Finally show a starting place. Use a crayon to trace a route to the 🎁 .

Your friend,

Buddy

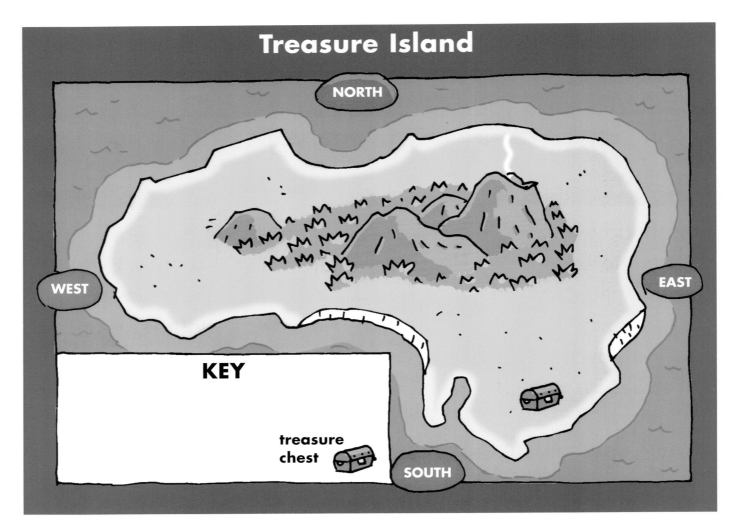

Treasure Island

NORTH

WEST

EAST

KEY

treasure chest

SOUTH

Let's Visit the Sea Park

Pretend you and your family are visiting the Sea Park. Follow the directions below to trace a route through the park.

☆ Use Your Skills

1. Go east from the Gate. Stop to buy tickets. Then go north to the first show. Circle it.

2. Go north to the next animal attraction. Draw a ✓ on it.

3. Head to the picnic tables. Turn and go north to see the next show. Draw a ★ on it.

4. Go east. Draw a line under the next show you see.

5. Go south past the hot dog stand. Then go west to the trash can. Now go south. What show will you see? Draw an ✗ on it.

Land and Water

Earth has many different kinds of land and water. Look at the pictures on these two pages. How many of these kinds of land and water have you seen before?

A **mountain** is the highest kind of land. Some mountains have snow at the top all year long.

A **hill** is land that is higher than the land around it. A hill is lower than a mountain.

A **plain** is flat land. Most plains are good for growing food.

 Think It Over

1. How are a mountain and a hill alike?
2. How are they different?

A **river** is a long body of water that flows across the land. A river usually flows into a lake or an ocean.

An **ocean** is a very large body of water. The water in an ocean is salty.

A **lake** is water with land all around it. A lake is smaller than an ocean. Most lakes have fresh water.

⭐ Use Your Skills

1. I'm the highest land on Earth. What am I?

   plain   mountain

2. I'm a body of water surrounded by land. What am I?

   lake   plain

3. I flow across the land. What am I?

   river   lake

Land and Water on a Map

Frog Lake

NORTH

EAST

WEST

SOUTH

KEY

River   Island   Mountain

Lake   Hill

Land and water can be shown as symbols on a map. Some symbols are colors. Water is usually shown as the color ▇▇▇ . Describe the symbol for a lake.

☆ Use Your Skills

1. What is the symbol for mountain? Draw a ★ on it on the map.

2. What does this symbol [hill symbol] stand for? _____ Draw a ✓ on it on the map.

3. Find the river on the map. Draw an ✗ on it.

4. Find the [island symbol] on the map. What surrounds it? _____

28

 **Map It!**

Now you can make your own land and water map. You can draw any kind of land and water you want on the map. Add some animals and houses if you want. Be sure to put everything in the key. Remember to include a title for your map.

Title

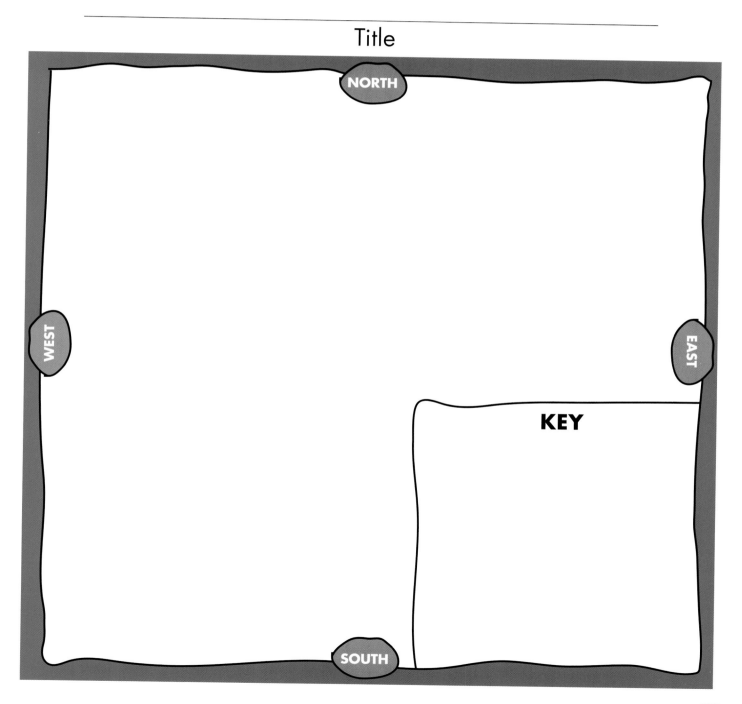

NORTH

WEST

EAST

KEY

SOUTH

Our World

The World

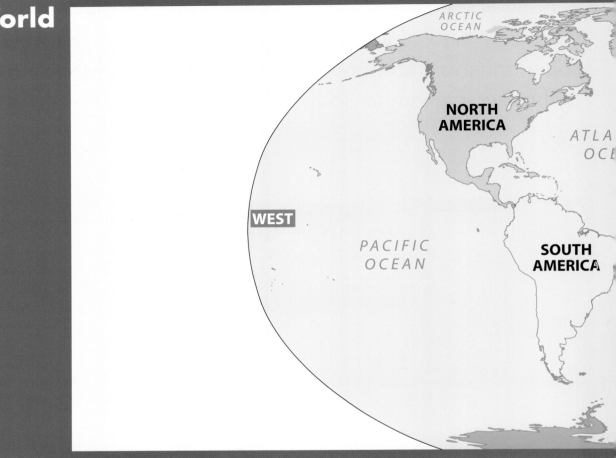

This map shows our whole world. The very large bodies of land are called **continents**. There are seven continents on Earth. What are their names?

Earth also has five oceans. You have read that an **ocean** is a very large body of salty water. Oceans cover most of Earth. Name the five oceans.

 Think It Over

What is the smallest continent? What continent is nearest to it?

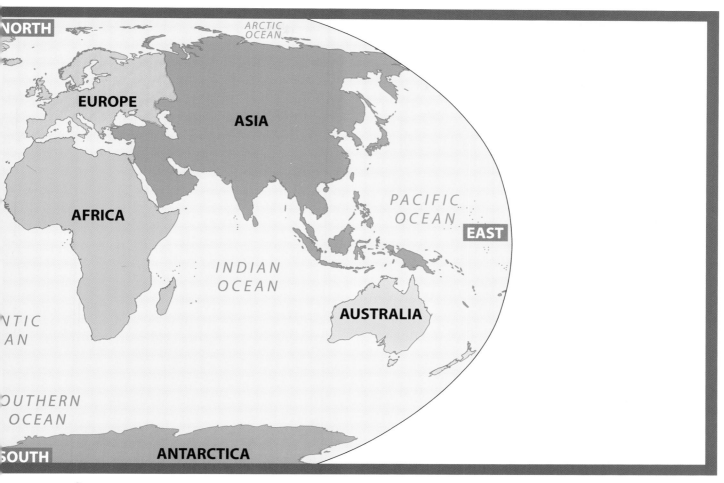

⭐ Use Your Skills

1. Find the Pacific Ocean labels on the map. How many are there? Circle them.

2. Draw a line under the Indian Ocean label. Is Asia north or south of the Indian Ocean? _____

3. Draw a ★ on the continents of Europe and Asia. Which continent is farther east? _____

4. Draw a ✔ on the continent of Africa. Which ocean is west of Africa? _____

Our Continent

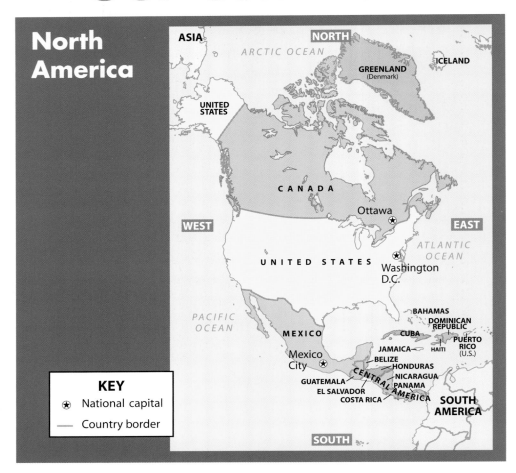

North America

KEY

★ National capital

— Country border

The continent we live on is called North America. Our continent has three large countries. A **country** is a land and the people who live there. North America also has some smaller countries. Some countries of North America are islands.

Every country has a border. A **border** tells where one place ends and another begins. Find the symbol for a country border in the map key. Then draw a ✓ on the border between the United States and Mexico.

 Think It Over

Look at the borders on the map. Do you think these lines are drawn on Earth too? Why or why not?

Three Large Countries

Our country is the United States. The national capital of our country is Washington, D.C. The national **capital** is where the leaders of a country work. Circle the of the United States on the map.

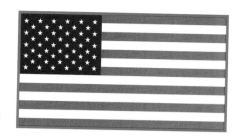

Canada is the country north of the United States. Draw a ✓ on the border between these two countries. Canada separates part of the United States from the rest of the country.

Put a ★ on the country of Mexico. In what direction is Mexico from the United States? Find the ⭐ for Mexico. What is the name of Mexico's national capital?

☆ Use Your Skills

Draw a line under the sentences that are true.

1. The Pacific Ocean is west of North America.
2. Ottawa is the national capital of Mexico.
3. Washington, D.C., is in the eastern United States.
4. The Atlantic Ocean is north of North America.
5. Canada includes many islands.
6. Mexico is south of the United States.

Our Country

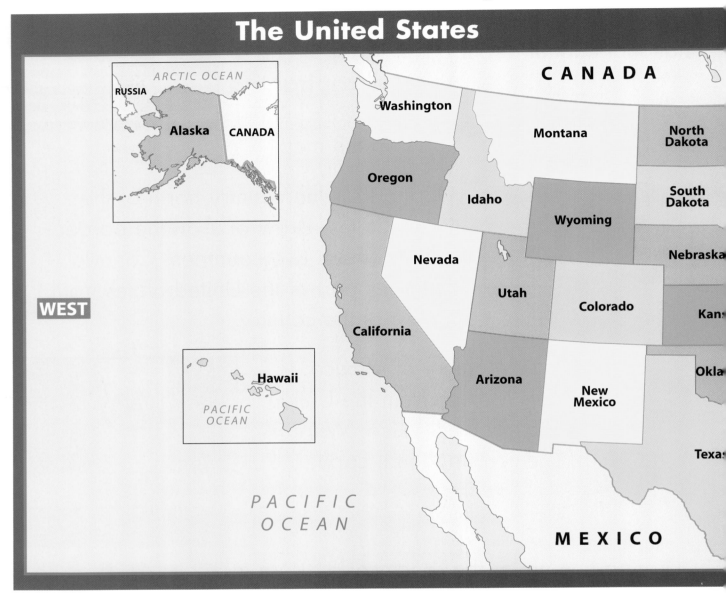

The United States

ARCTIC OCEAN

RUSSIA

Alaska

CANADA

CANADA

Washington

Montana

North Dakota

Oregon

Idaho

South Dakota

Wyoming

WEST

Nevada

Nebraska

Utah

Colorado

Kan

California

Hawaii

PACIFIC OCEAN

Arizona

New Mexico

Okla

Texa

PACIFIC OCEAN

MEXICO

The country we live in is called the United States. The United States is a big country. It is made up of 50 states. A **state** is part of a country. Every state has a border. Look at the map key to see the difference between a state border and a country border.

Most states in the United States are right next to other states. But two states, Alaska and Hawaii, are far away from all the other states.

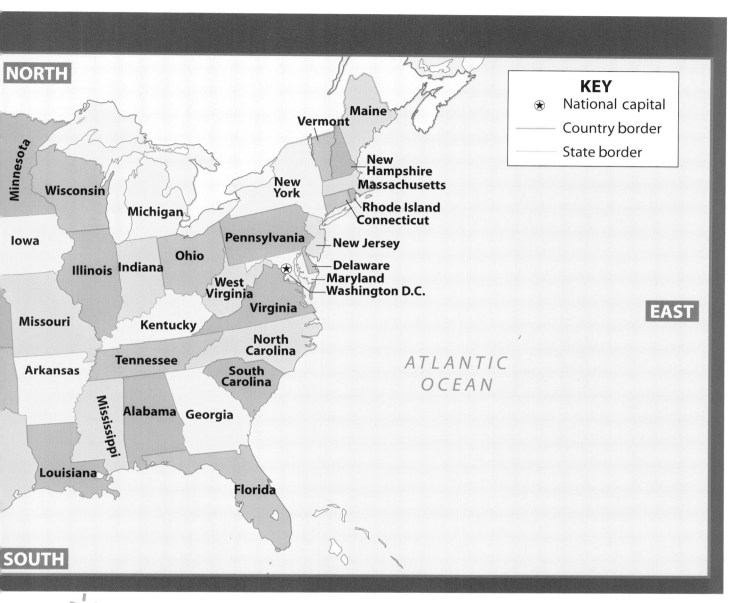

Use Your Skills

1. Find your state and draw a ✔on it.

2. Draw a ★ on all the states that share a border with your state. How many states border your state? _____

3. Utah is _____ of Arizona.

4. Colorado is _____ of Kansas.

5. Ohio is _____ of Indiana.

A Visit to California

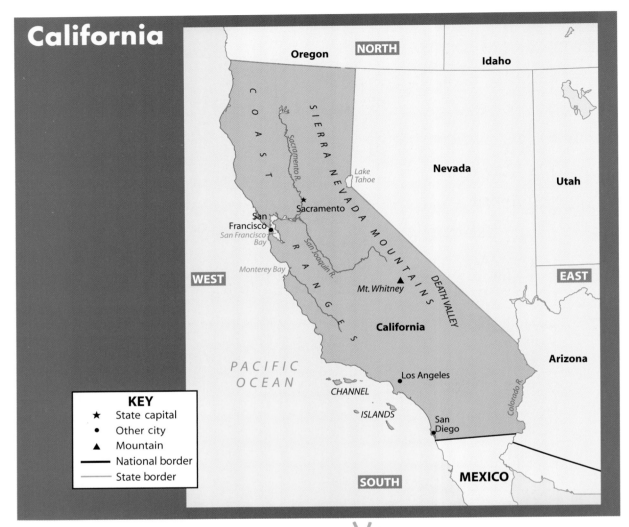

California

KEY
- ★ State capital
- ● Other city
- ▲ Mountain
- ▬ National border
- ▬ State border

Oregon · NORTH · Idaho · Nevada · Utah · COAST · SIERRA NEVADA MOUNTAINS · Sacramento R. · Lake Tahoe · Sacramento · San Francisco · San Francisco Bay · WEST · Monterey Bay · RANGES · San Joaquin R. · Mt. Whitney · DEATH VALLEY · California · EAST · Arizona · PACIFIC OCEAN · Los Angeles · Colorado R. · CHANNEL · ISLANDS · San Diego · SOUTH · MEXICO

The state of California is one of the largest states in the United States. More people live in California than in any other state in our country.

Think It Over

California has borders with other states. It also has a border with another country. Draw a ★ on the country border. What country has a border with California? Draw a ✔ on the state borders. What states have borders with California?

36

Land and Water in California

The capital of California is Sacramento. The leaders of the state meet there. Find the symbol ★ in the map key. What does it stand for? Circle it on the map.

California has many high mountains. Mount Whitney is one of the highest mountains in the United States. Draw a ★ on Mount Whitney.

There are many lakes in California. Lake Tahoe is on the border between California and Nevada. Draw a ✓ on the lake. The water is very blue. If you put your hand in the water, you'll find out that it's very cold!

☆ Use Your Skills

Use the map to complete the sentences.

1. The California city closest to Mexico on the map is

   _____.

2. The Pacific Ocean is _____ of California.

3. The city of San Francisco is _____ of the city of Los Angeles.

4. The _____ mountains are located near the Pacific Ocean.

A Visit to Virginia

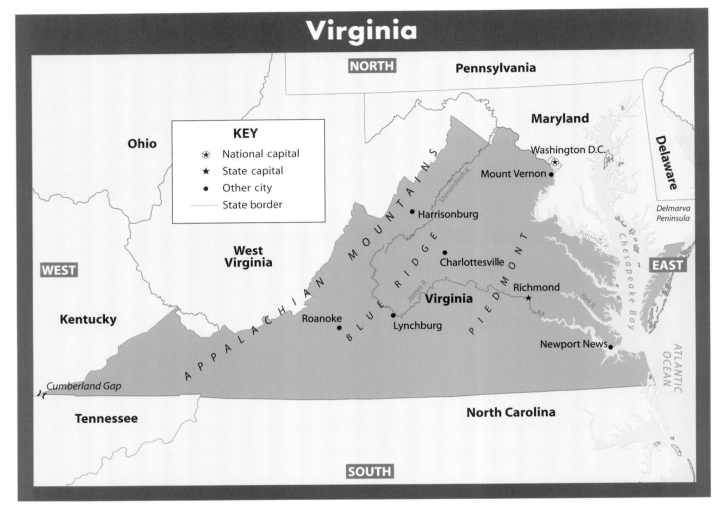

Virginia

NORTH Pennsylvania

Ohio

Maryland

Washington D.C.

Delaware

KEY
★ National capital
★ State capital
● Other city
— State border

Delmarva Peninsula

West Virginia

Mount Vernon

APPALACHIAN MOUNTAINS

Shenandoah R.

Harrisonburg

WEST

Charlottesville

BLUE RIDGE

Virginia

Richmond

PIEDMONT

Potomac R.

Chesapeake Bay

EAST

Kentucky

James R.

Roanoke

Lynchburg

York R.

Newport News

ATLANTIC OCEAN

Cumberland Gap

Tennessee

North Carolina

SOUTH

Virginia is a state in the eastern part of the United States. It was one of the first 13 states of our country. George Washington, the first president of the United States, was born in Virginia. You can visit his home at Mount Vernon.

Your Turn Now

Many other presidents also came from Virginia. Use the library or Internet to make a list. Find out where their homes are in Virginia.

Land and Water in Virginia

The capital of Virginia is Richmond. Draw a circle around its symbol on the map. Draw a line under the symbol for Washington, D.C. What two states share a border with the capital of the United States?

Virginia's mountains are not as high as the mountains in California. Find some of Virginia's mountains on the map. Draw an ✗ on them.

A small part of Virginia is separated from the rest of the state. It is part of the Delmarva peninsula. A **peninsula** is land surrounded on three sides by water. Draw a ✓on the Delmarva peninsula.

Use Your Skills

Underline the sentences that are true.

1. The capital city of Virginia is Sacramento.

2. Virginia is in the eastern part of the United States.

3. The Atlantic Ocean is east of Virginia.

Think It Over

What are the three states that are part of the Delmarva peninsula? How do you think the peninsula got its name?

A Visit to Canada

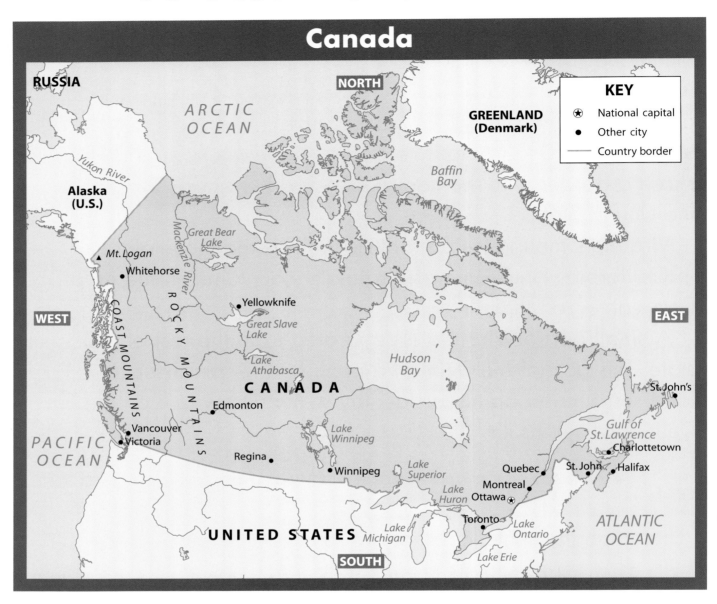

Canada is our neighbor to the north. It is much larger than the United States. But it has fewer people. Canada goes very far north. The northern parts of the country are cold all year long.

 **Think It Over**

Why do you think most of Canada's cities are located in the southern part of the country?

Meet Canada's People

Canada

Languages:
English and French
Capital: Ottawa

Hello/Bonjour

Canada's people are like the people in the United States. They have come from all over the world.

Many languages are spoken in Canada. But English and French are both official languages. That means that many signs in Canada are written in English and French.

⭐ Use Your Skills

1. Circle Canada's capital city on the map. Is it in the north or the south? _____

2. Draw an ✗ on the names of the oceans that touch Canada. How many are there? _____

3. Draw a ★ on each of the five lakes between Canada and the United States. What are they called?

   _____

   _____

4. Draw a ✓ on the two borders that Canada shares with the United States. Which state is north of most of Canada? _____

A Visit to Mexico

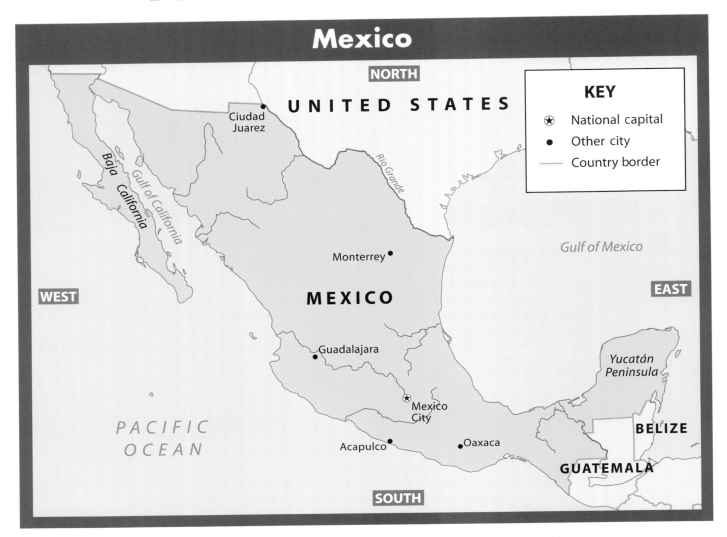

Mexico is our neighbor to the south. It is a smaller country than the United States. Mexico is warmer and drier too.

Find the Rio Grande on the map. Draw a ✔on it. This river forms part of the border between Mexico and the United States.

Your Turn Now

Look at a globe or a map of North America. Find the continent of North America. Name the two countries that border Mexico on the south.

Meet Mexico's People

Mexico

Language:
Spanish
Capital:
Mexico City

Hola

Mexicans, like people in the United States and Canada, live mostly in cities. The capital city of Mexico is Mexico City. Draw a circle around its symbol on the map.

Use Your Skills

Circle the place that completes each sentence.

1. The Rio Grande forms part of the border between Mexico and _____.

   the United States   **Canada**

2. The capital city of Mexico is _____.

   Mexico City   **Ottawa**

3. The city of _____ is in northern Mexico.

   Oaxaca   **Ciudad Juarez**

Putting It All Together

Dear Girls and Boys,
    Here's a map of a new town. Many people will live, shop, play, go to school, and work here. The streets have been built. There is also an airport and a railroad.

Title

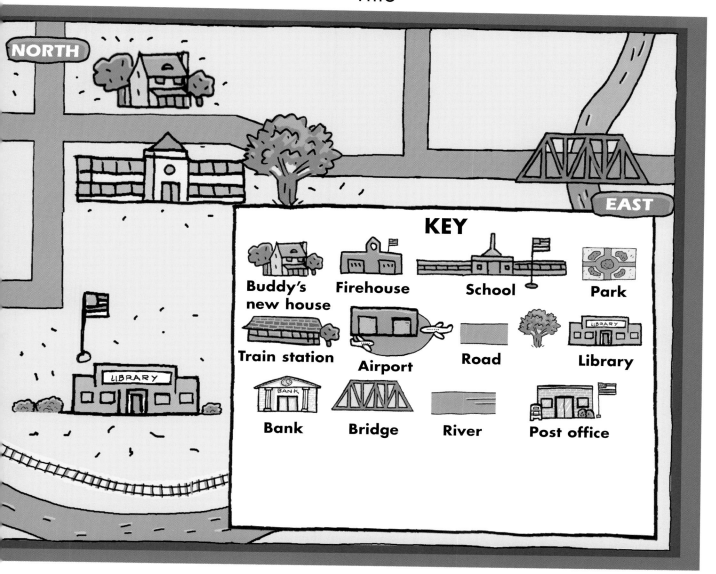

KEY

Buddy's new house   Firehouse   School   Park

Train station   Airport   Road   Library

Bank   Bridge   River   Post office

The key has symbols for the places already on the map. It also has symbols for things you can place anywhere you want on the map. You can also draw your own symbols in the key for things you want to add to the map. Don't forget to name the town!

Your friend,

Buddy

Reviewing Map Skills

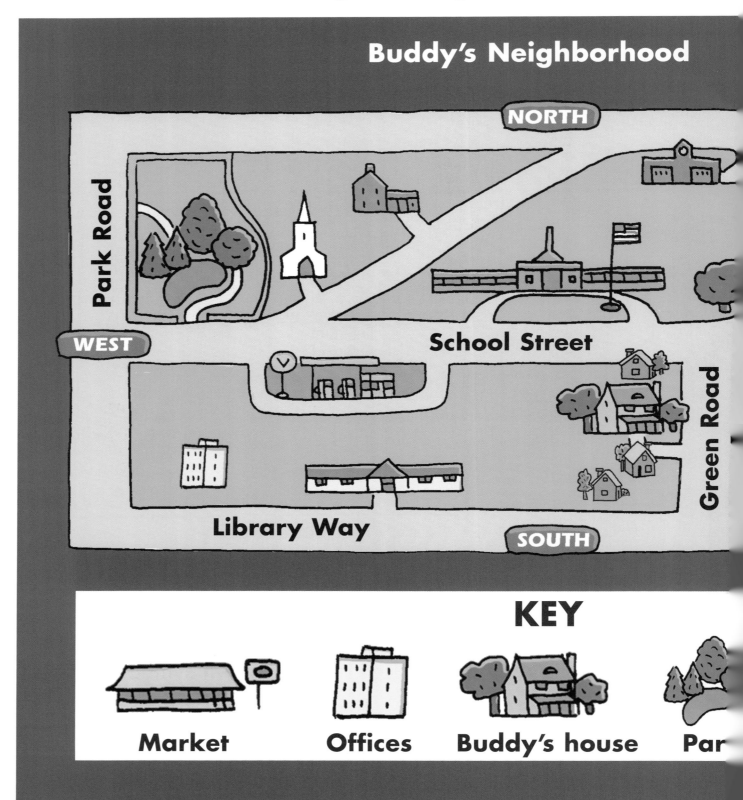

Buddy's Neighborhood

NORTH

Park Road

WEST

School Street

Green Road

Library Way

SOUTH

KEY

Market   Offices   Buddy's house   Par

EAST

School

Circle the correct answer to finish each sentence.

1. This symbol [symbol] stands for

   _____.

   offices   **house**

2. The park is on the _____ side of the map.

   left   **right**

3. Trace the shortest route from the school to Buddy's house. The directions you went are _____.

   east and south

   west and north

Notes